SEASHORE
Activity Book

Patricia J. Wynne

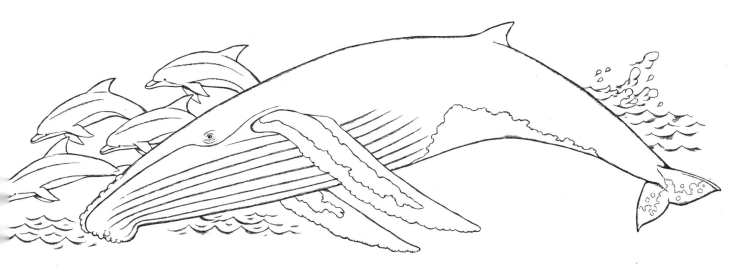

DOVER PUBLICATIONS, INC.
Mineola, New York

Publisher's Note

The seashore is teeming with life, both seen and unseen. There are shore birds walking on the sand, looking for crabs, snails, and worms to eat. Seaweed can be spotted at the water's edge, moving in and out with the tides. Dolphins soar into the air far out at sea. Small creatures such as seahorses, periwinkles, and pea crabs may not be easy to spot. And flounders and angel sharks are all but invisible as they lie on the sea floor or swim underwater.

Walk along the shoreline, and you will be amazed by the sights, sounds, and smells of the sea and its incredibly varied inhabitants. In this book, you will learn about the various animals and habitats of the seashore. There are puzzles to do, and pages to color. There's even a "Seashore Sketchbook" (pages 25 through 30), where you can try your hand at drawing sea creatures such as a manatee and a Great White shark. A Solutions section appears on pages 41 through 46, in case you need to check your answers. Enjoy your visit!

Copyright

Copyright © 2006, 2013 by Dover Publications, Inc.
All rights reserved.

Bibliographical Note

BOOST Seashore Activity Book, first published by Dover Publications, Inc., in 2013, is a revised edition of *Seashore Activity Book*, originally published by Dover in 2006.

International Standard Book Number
ISBN-13: 978-0-486-49408-1
ISBN-10: 0-486-49408-X

Manufactured in the United States by Courier Corporation
49408X01   2013
www.doverpublications.com

The seashore is crowded. A horseshoe crab scuttles across the beach.
The bird looks for clams and snails.

 RI.1.1 Ask and answer questions about key details in a text. Also **RI.1.3, RI.1.7, RF.1.4;**
RI.2.1, RI.2.3, RI.2.7, RF.2.4.

1

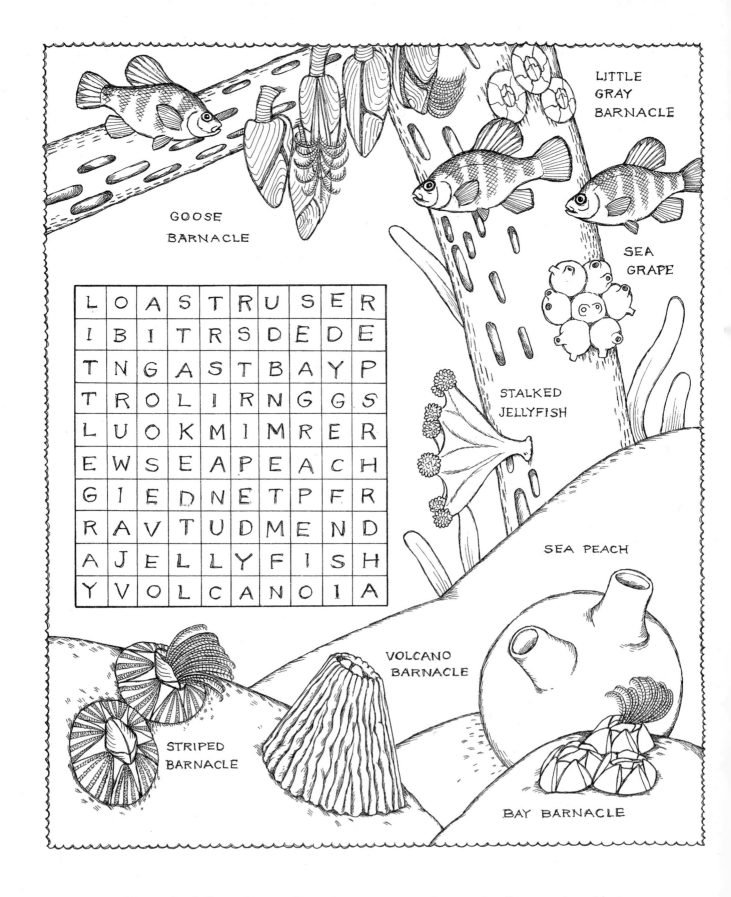

LITTLE GRAY BARNACLE

GOOSE BARNACLE

SEA GRAPE

STALKED JELLYFISH

SEA PEACH

VOLCANO BARNACLE

STRIPED BARNACLE

BAY BARNACLE

L	O	A	S	T	R	U	S	E	R
I	B	I	T	R	S	D	E	D	E
T	N	G	A	S	T	B	A	Y	P
T	R	O	L	I	R	N	G	G	S
L	U	O	K	M	I	M	R	E	R
E	W	S	E	A	P	E	A	C	H
G	I	E	D	N	E	T	P	F	R
R	A	V	T	U	D	M	E	N	D
A	J	E	L	L	Y	F	I	S	H
Y	V	O	L	C	A	N	O	I	A

Many animals live underwater. Barnacles, sea grapes, and sea peaches live on sunken objects. They catch food as it drifts by. Find the names of the creatures.

These are coquina clams. Their shells protect their bodies. Their tubes pull and push water.
Find two coquina shells that are exactly alike.

 RI.1.6 Distinguish between information provided by pictures or other illustrations and information provided by the words in a text. Also **RI.1.2, RI.1.4; RI.2.4, RI.2.6.**

3

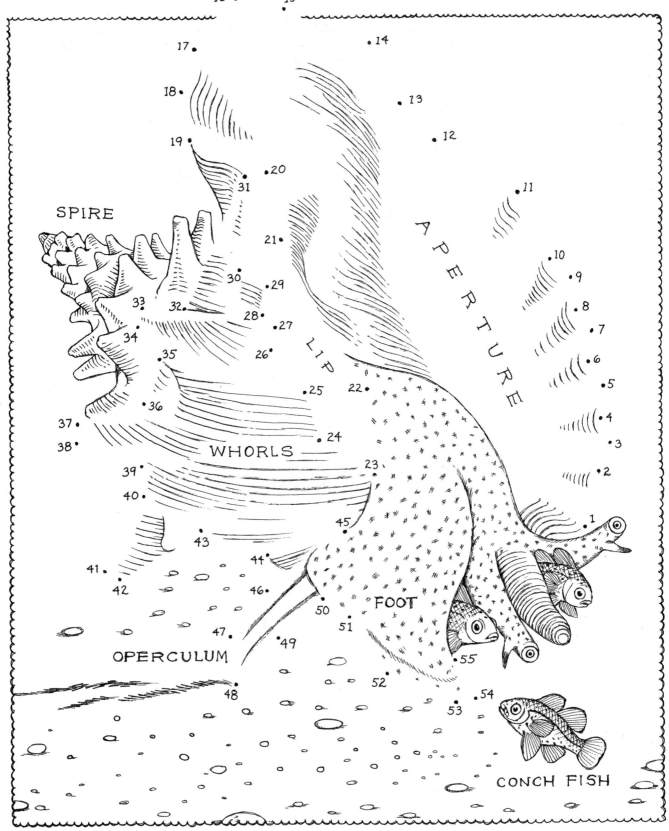

SPIRE

APERTURE

LIP

WHORLS

OPERCULUM

FOOT

CONCH FISH

This is a queen conch. It is a big snail. It can grow as big as a soccer ball!
The conch can go inside its shell. Connect the dots to see the queen conch.

 RI.1.4 Ask and answer questions to help determine or clarify the meaning of words and phrases in a text. Also **RI.1.7, L.1.4.a; RI.2.4, RI.2.7, L.2.4.a.**

START

FINISH

Sea otters hunt for food in seaweed. They like snails, clams, and urchins.
Otters eat off of their stomachs. Help the otter find its way.

RI.1.2 Identify the main topic and retell key details of a text. Also **RI.1.6, RI.1.10; RI.2.6, RI.2.10.**

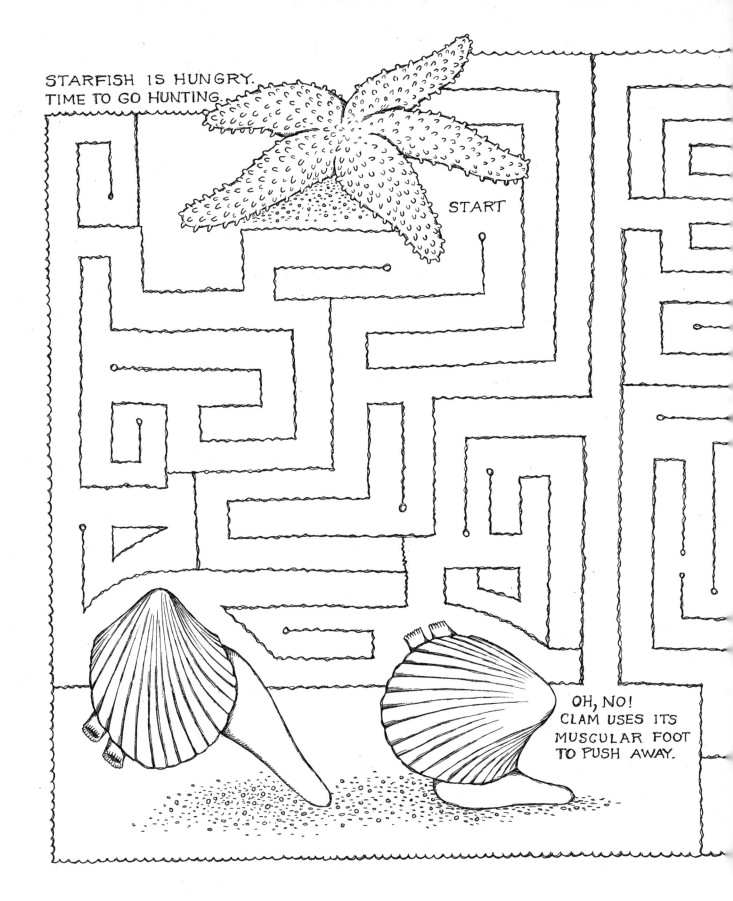

STARFISH IS HUNGRY.
TIME TO GO HUNTING.

START

OH, NO!
CLAM USES ITS
MUSCULAR FOOT
TO PUSH AWAY.

The starfish hunts for clams and scallops. It uses its arms to open the shells.
Help the starfish find its dinner.

 CCSS **RI.1.1** Ask and answer questions about key details in a text. Also **RI.1.3, RI.1.7, RF.1.4.a;**
RI.2.1, RI.2.3, RI.2.7, RF.2.4.a, L.2.4.d.

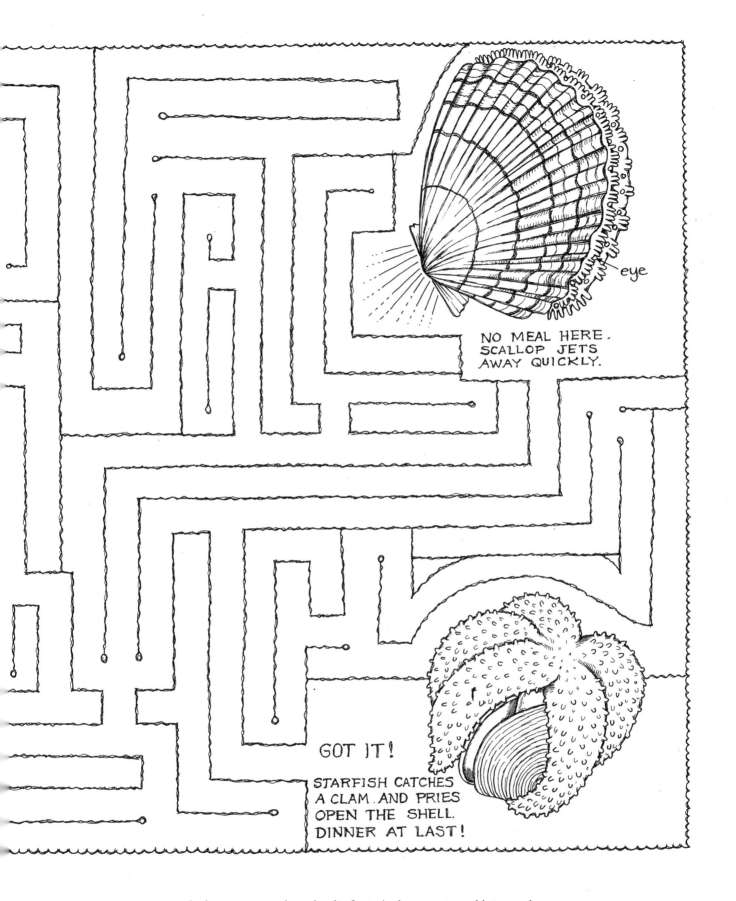

eye

NO MEAL HERE.
SCALLOP JETS
AWAY QUICKLY.

GOT IT!

STARFISH CATCHES
A CLAM. AND PRIES
OPEN THE SHELL.
DINNER AT LAST!

A clam can move by using its foot. A clam can tunnel into sand.
A scallop can "jet away" by squirting water.

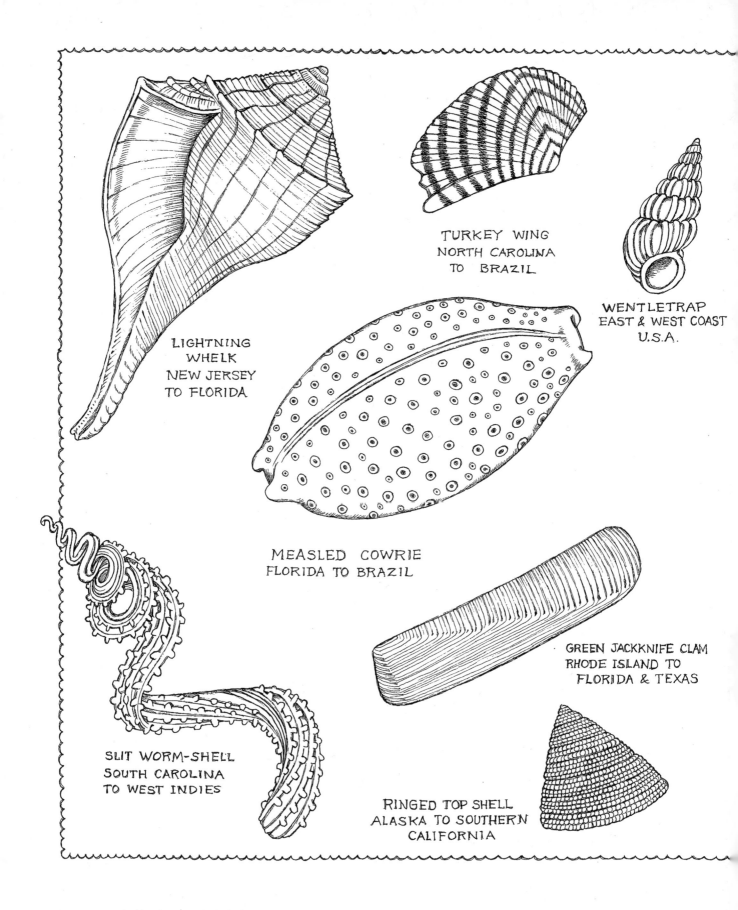

LIGHTNING
WHELK
NEW JERSEY
TO FLORIDA

TURKEY WING
NORTH CAROLINA
TO BRAZIL

WENTLETRAP
EAST & WEST COAST
U.S.A.

MEASLED COWRIE
FLORIDA TO BRAZIL

GREEN JACKKNIFE CLAM
RHODE ISLAND TO
FLORIDA & TEXAS

SLIT WORM-SHELL
SOUTH CAROLINA
TO WEST INDIES

RINGED TOP SHELL
ALASKA TO SOUTHERN
CALIFORNIA

Collecting seashells is fun! Walk along the beach. You will find shells. Carry your shells in a bag.

RI.1.2 Identify the main topic and retell key details of a text. Also **RI.1.4, RI.1.5, RI.1.7, L.1.6; RI.2.2, RI.2.4, RI.2.5, RI.2.7, L.2.4.d, L.2.6.**

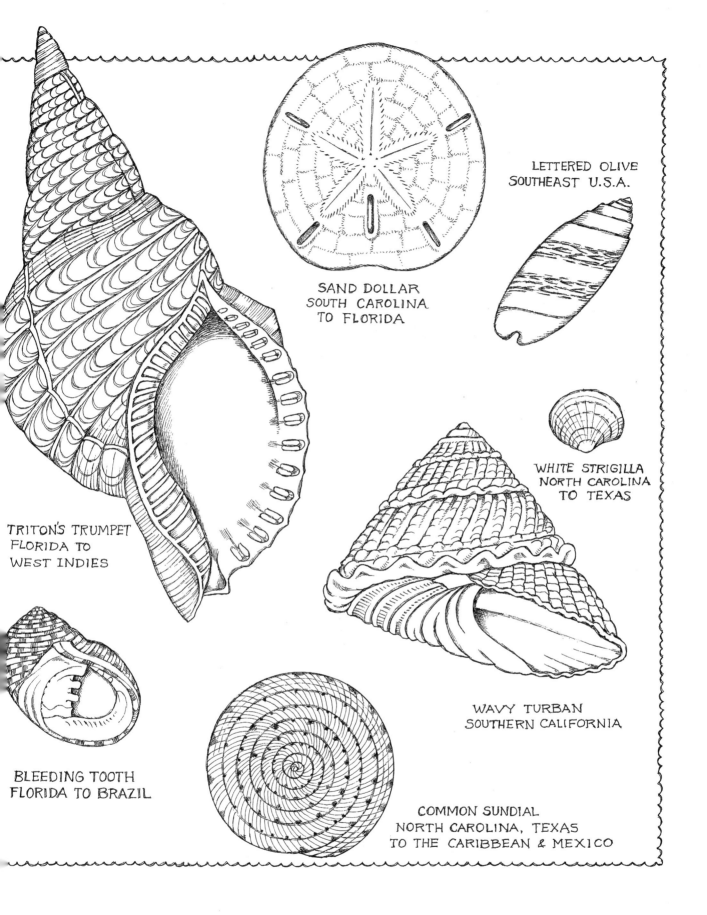

SAND DOLLAR
SOUTH CAROLINA
TO FLORIDA

LETTERED OLIVE
SOUTHEAST U.S.A.

WHITE STRIGILLA
NORTH CAROLINA
TO TEXAS

TRITON'S TRUMPET
FLORIDA TO
WEST INDIES

WAVY TURBAN
SOUTHERN CALIFORNIA

BLEEDING TOOTH
FLORIDA TO BRAZIL

COMMON SUNDIAL
NORTH CAROLINA, TEXAS
TO THE CARIBBEAN & MEXICO

Throw closed shells back into the water. Be careful. There might be a living animal inside.

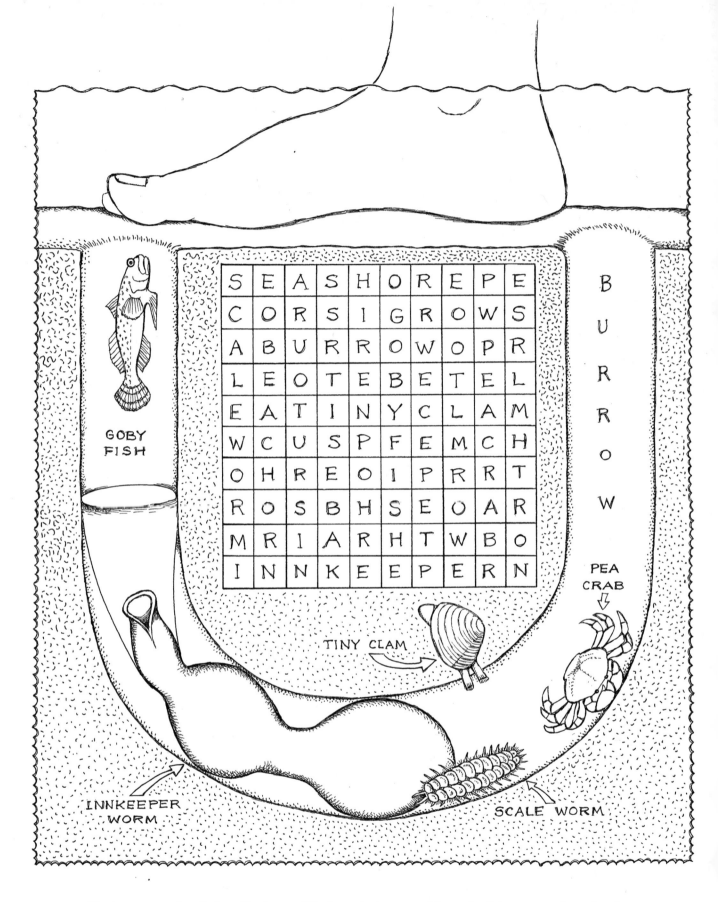

The large worm is called an "innkeeper." It shares its burrow with a goby fish, a pea crab, and a clam.
Circle the animal names in the puzzle.

 RI.1.3 Describe the connection between two individuals, events, ideas, or pieces of information in a text. Also **RI.1.5, RI.1.7; RI.2.3, RI.2.5, RI.2.7, L.2.4.d.**

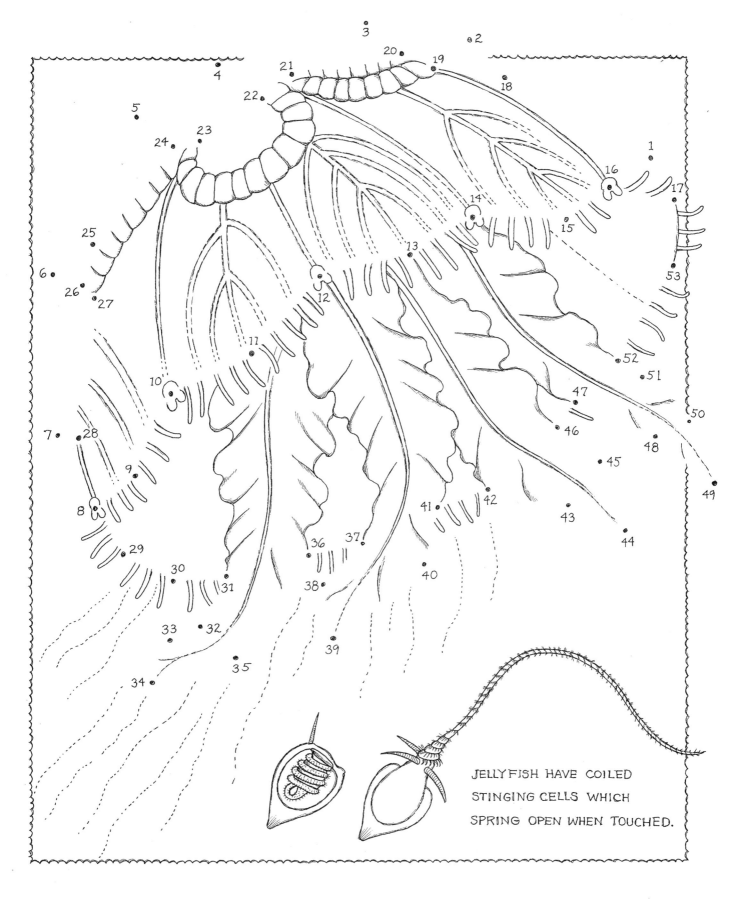

JELLYFISH HAVE COILED
STINGING CELLS WHICH
SPRING OPEN WHEN TOUCHED.

Jellyfish look gentle, but be careful! Their tentacles can burn you.
Connect the dots to see the moon jellyfish.

 CCSS **RI.1.6** Distinguish between information provided by pictures or other illustrations and information provided by the words in a text. Also **RI.1.4, RI.1.7, RF.1.3.a; RI.2.4, RI.2.6, RI.2.7, L.2.4.d.**

Why do birds like the seashore? Birds eat fish, clams, crabs, snails, and worms.
Use the code on page 13 to spell the names of these birds.

2 11 1 3 10

17 10 9 12 12 5 16

1 16 3 18 9 3

18 5 16 13

17 1 13 4 15 9 15 5 16 17

17 1 13 4 5 16 11 9 13 7

15 9 15 9 13 7

15 11 14 20 5 16

A	B	C	D	E	F	G	H	I	K	L	M	N	O	P	R	S	T	U	V	W	Y
1	2	3	4	5	6	7	8	9	10	11	12	13	14	15	16	17	18	19	20	21	22

A bird's beak is a tool. Birds' beaks help them get food. Some beaks are good for sand.
Some beaks are good for mud. Some beaks are good for water.

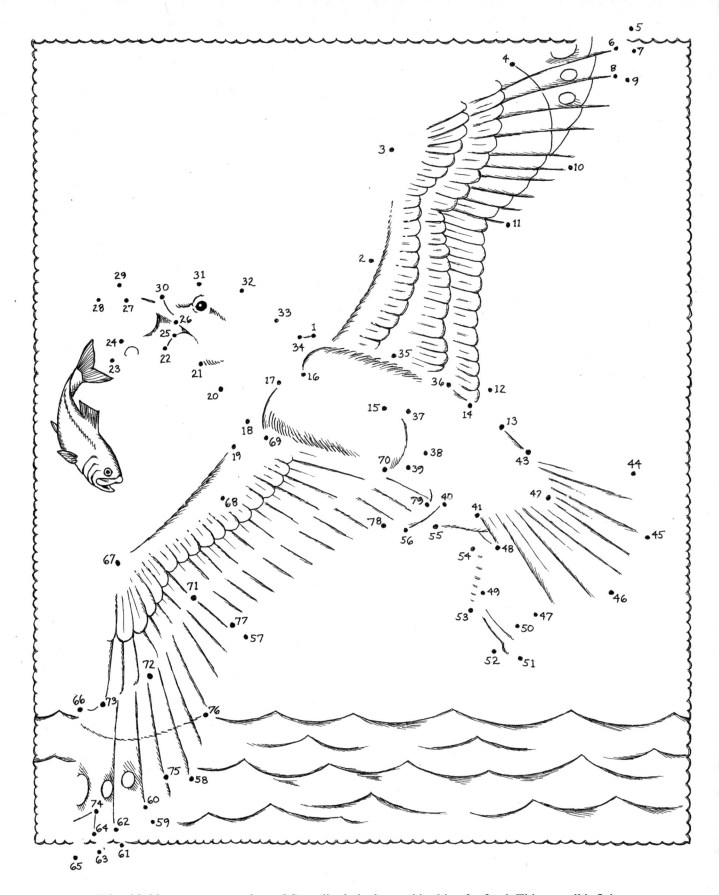

What bird is common near the sea? Seagulls circle the sand looking for food. This seagull is flying.
It dropped a fish. Connect the dots to see the seagull.

RI.1.7 Use the illustrations and details in a text to describe its key ideas. Also **RI.1.1, RI.1.6; RI.2.1, RI.2.6, RI.2.7.**

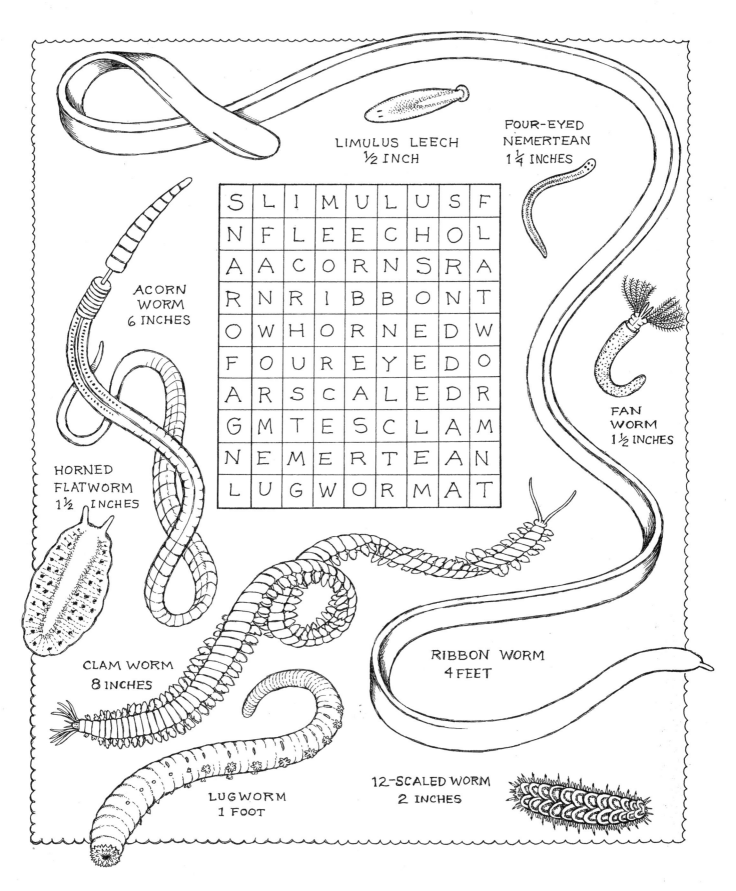

LIMULUS LEECH
½ INCH

FOUR-EYED
NEMERTEAN
1 ¼ INCHES

ACORN
WORM
6 INCHES

FAN
WORM
1 ½ INCHES

HORNED
FLATWORM
1 ½ INCHES

CLAM WORM
8 INCHES

RIBBON WORM
4 FEET

LUGWORM
1 FOOT

12-SCALED WORM
2 INCHES

The word search grid:

S	L	I	M	U	L	U	S	F
N	F	L	E	E	C	H	O	L
A	A	C	O	R	N	S	R	A
R	N	R	I	B	B	O	N	T
O	W	H	O	R	N	E	D	W
F	O	U	R	E	Y	E	D	O
A	R	S	C	A	L	E	D	R
G	M	T	E	S	C	L	A	M
N	E	M	E	R	T	E	A	N
L	U	G	W	O	R	M	A	T

Worms live at the seashore. Some grow to be very long. Some glow in the dark.
Circle the names of these worms.

RI.1.6 Distinguish between information provided by pictures or other illustrations and information provided by the words in a text. Also **RI.1.5, RF.1.4; RI.2.5, RI.2.6, RF.2.4, L.2.4.d.**

15

Some seashores are rocky. This seashore has orange starfish, red snails, and purple crabs.
Color this busy shore scene.

 RI.1.2 Identify the main topic and retell key details of a text. Also **RI.1.7, RF.1.3.a, L.1.6; RI.2.7, RF.2.3.c, L.2.6.**

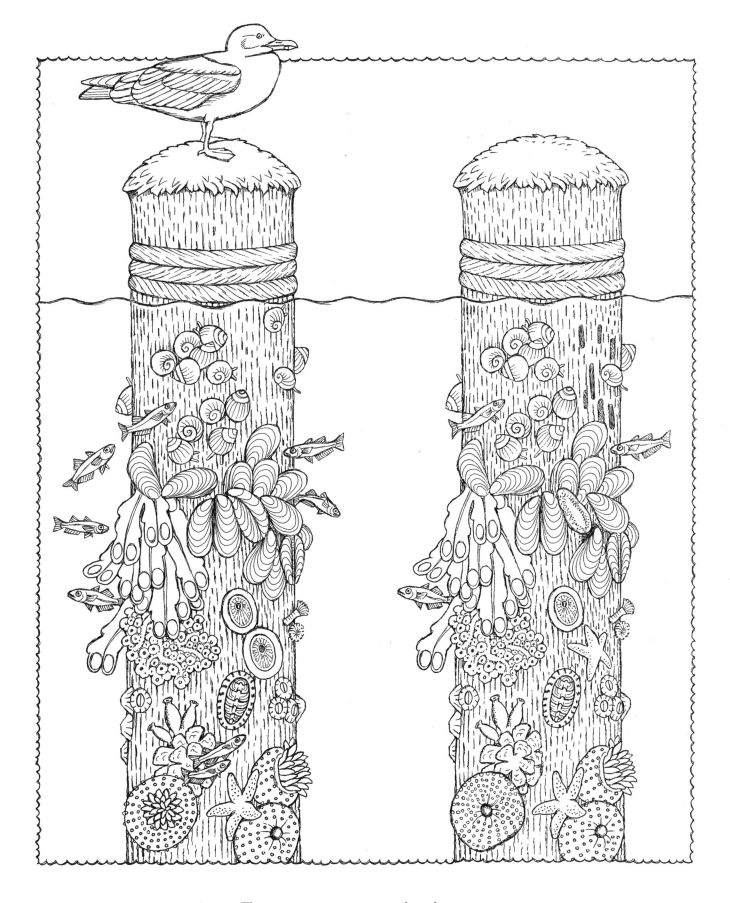

There are many creatures stuck to these posts.
Circle the eight things that are different on the right post.

 RI.1.9 Identify basic similarities in and differences between two texts on the same topic.
Also **RI.1.1, RI.1.7, SL.1.2; RI.2.1, RI.2.7, RI.2.9, SL.2.2.**

17

Mangrove trees grow on the Florida coast. Birds called ibises perch on the branches.
Other animals live on the mangroves. Can you spot the manatees nearby?

  RI.1.2 Identify the main topic and retell key details of a text. Also **RI.1.4, RI.1.6, RF.1.4,
SL.1.2; RI.2.4, RI.2.6, RF.2.4, SL.2.2.**

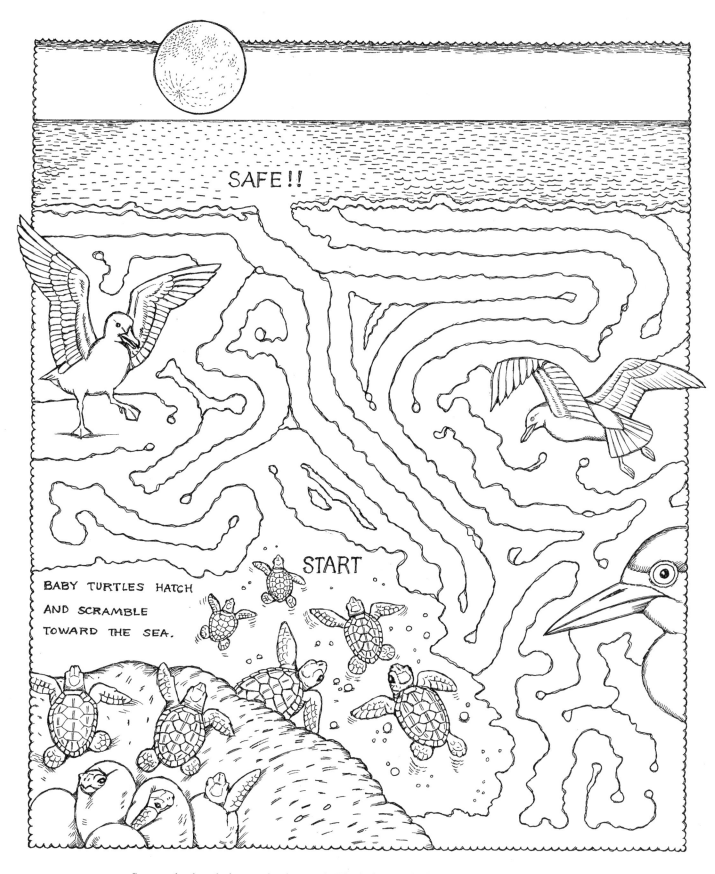

SAFE!!

START

BABY TURTLES HATCH
AND SCRAMBLE
TOWARD THE SEA.

Sea turtles lay their eggs in the sand. The baby turtles hatch. They crawl to the sea.
Help the baby turtles to the sea.

RI.1.3 Describe the connection between two individuals, events, ideas, or pieces of information in a text. Also **RI.1.1, RI.1.7, SL.1.2; RI.2.1, RI.2.7, SL.2.2.**

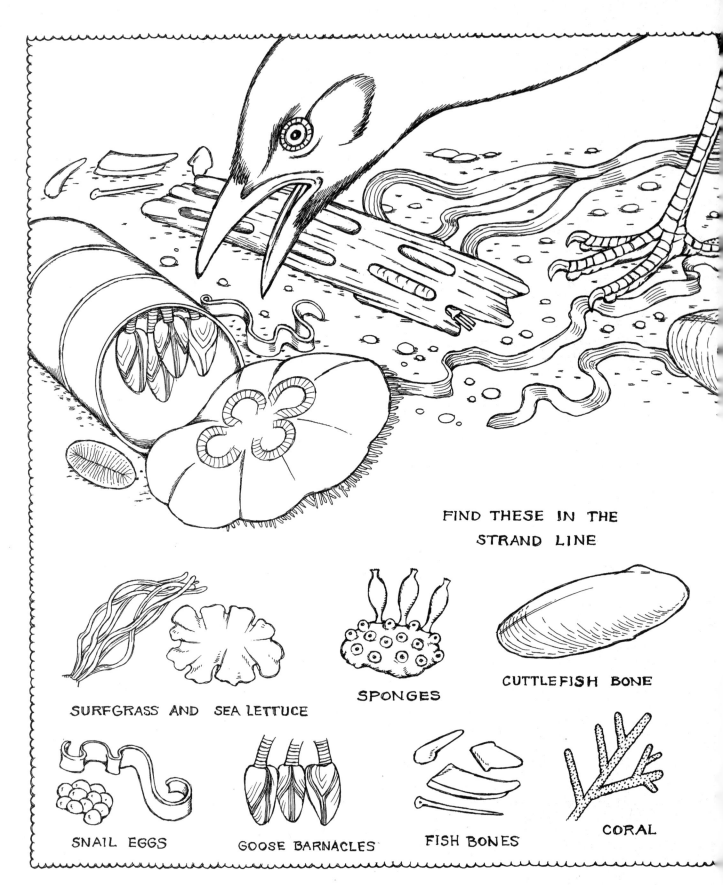

FIND THESE IN THE
STRAND LINE

SURFGRASS AND SEA LETTUCE

SPONGES

CUTTLEFISH BONE

SNAIL EGGS

GOOSE BARNACLES

FISH BONES

CORAL

A strandline is made by the waves. Many things are found along the strandline.
Find these pictures in the strandline.

RI.1.2 Identify the main topic and retell key details of a text. Also **RI.1.4, RI.1.5, L.1.6;
RI.2.2, RI.2.4, RI.2.5, L.2.6.**

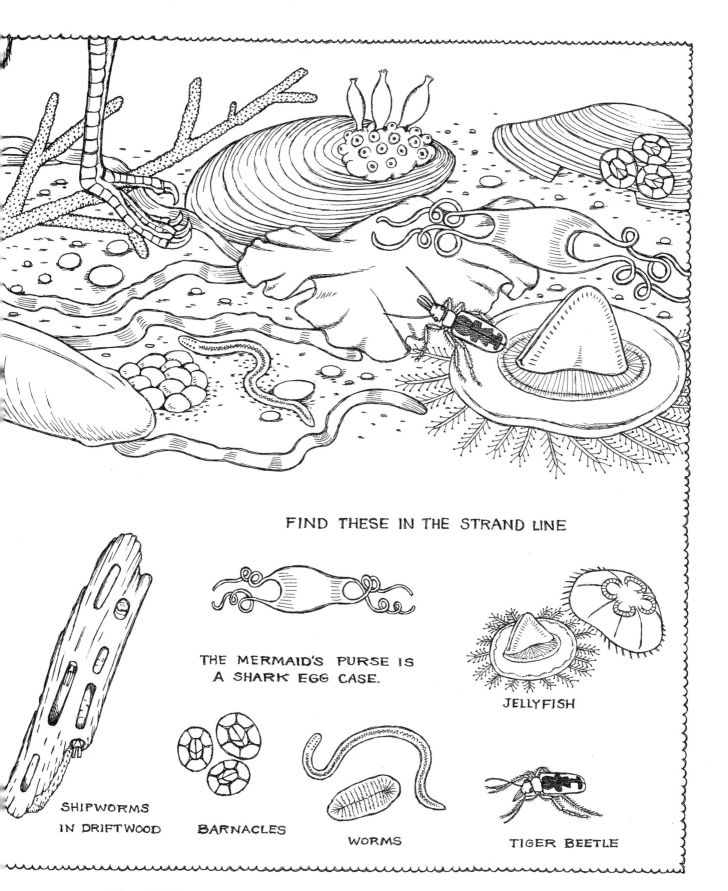

FIND THESE IN THE STRAND LINE

THE MERMAID'S PURSE IS
A SHARK EGG CASE.

JELLYFISH

SHIPWORMS
IN DRIFTWOOD

BARNACLES

WORMS

TIGER BEETLE

The seabird is searching the strandline. It may find a shark's egg case, driftwood, fish bones, or a can with barnacles. Find each of these pictures in the strandline.

2 13 17 17 10 5 12 13 16 5

4 13 10 14 7 8 12 16

11 1 12 1 17 5 5

12 13 15 17 7 5 15 12

16 5 1   10 8 13 12

A	B	C	D	E	H	I	K	L	M	N	O	P	R	S	T	U	W
1	2	3	4	5	7	8	9	10	11	12	13	14	15	16	17	18	19

Out in sea you can spot an otter, dolphins, a seal, a sea lion, a manatee, a whale, and a porpoise.
Use the code to spell the names of these sea creatures.

CCSS RI.1.7 Use the illustrations and details in a text to describe its key ideas. Also **RI.1.1, RI.1.4, RF.1.3.c, RF.1.3.f; RI.2.1, RI.2.4, RI.2.7.**

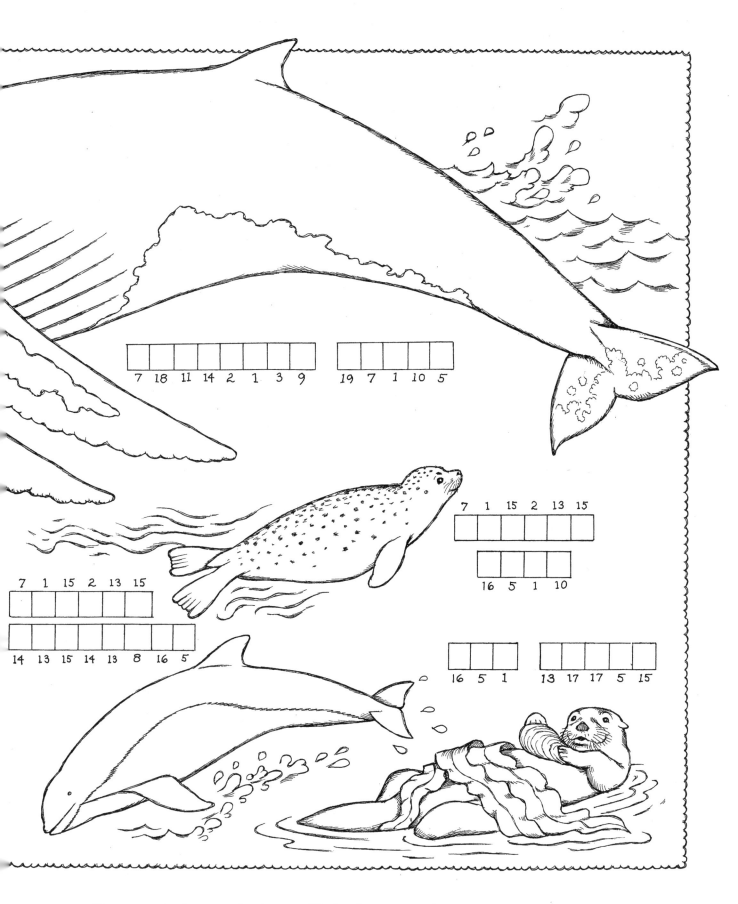

7	18	11	14	2	1	3	9

19	7	1	10	5

7	1	15	2	13	15

16	5	1	10

7	1	15	2	13	15

14	13	15	14	13	8	16	5

16	5	1

13	17	17	5	15

These sea animals are good swimmers. Whales shoot spouts of water in the air when they breathe.

Find the hidden animals swimming with the dolphins.
Can you find a seal, a sea bird, a girl wearing flippers, a shark, a ray, a fish, and a sea turtle?

 RI.1.1 Ask and answer questions about key details in a text. Also **RI.1.4, RI.1.7, RF.1.4; RI.2.1, RI.2.4, RI.2.7, RF.2.4.**

1   2   3   4   5

Seashore Sketchbook ~ Brown Pelican

Brown pelicans live on the Florida shore. This pelican has brown, yellow, and white feathers.
The beak is gray. Now draw your own pelican.

 RI.1.2 Identify the main topic and retell key details of a text. Also **RI.1.4, RI.1.6, RI.1.10; RI.2.3, RI.2.4, RI.2.6, RI.2.10, L.2.4.d.**

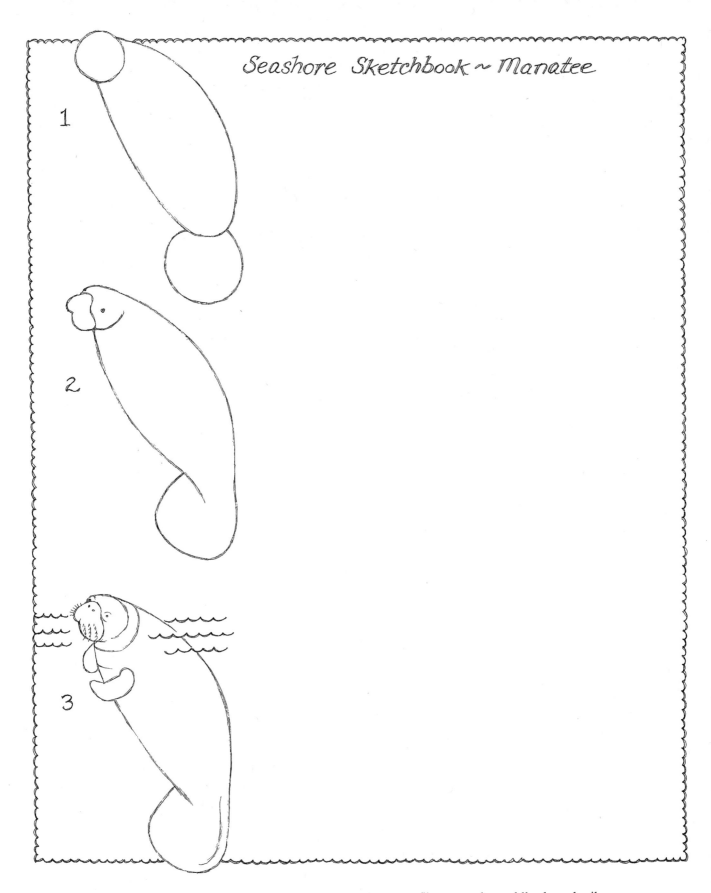

1

2

3

Manatees can grow up to ten feet long. They have two flippers and a paddle-shaped tail.
Draw your own manatee. Color it gray with a green back. The green is algae.

CCSS **RI.1.10** With prompting and support, read informational texts appropriately complex for
grade 1. Also **RI.1.4, RI.1.6, RF.1.4; RI.2.3, RI.2.4, RI.2.6, RI.2.10, RF.2.4.**

1

2

3

4

Seashore Sketchbook ~ Humpback Whale

Humpback whales can grow up to fifty feet long. Humpback whales leap out of the water.
Draw your own humpback whale. Color it gray and white.

 CCSS **RI.1.2** Identify the main topic and retell key details of a text. Also **RI.1.1, RI.1.6, RF.1.4; RI.2.1, RI.2.3, RI.2.6, RF.2.4, L.2.4.d.**

Seashore Sketchbook ~ Fighting Conch Shell

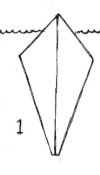

1

2

3

4

5

The fighting conch is a sea snail. It lives on shores from North Carolina to Texas.
They have a brown-and-white shell. Draw your own fighting conch.

 RI.1.4 Ask and answer questions to help determine or clarify the meaning of words and phrases in a text. Also **RI.1.2, RI.1.6, RI.1.10; RI.2.2, RI.2.3, RI.2.6, RI.2.10.**

Seashore Sketchbook ~ Seahorse

1

2

3

4

The sea horse is a small fish. It has fins, scales, and gills. Draw your own sea horse.
Color it yellow or orange.

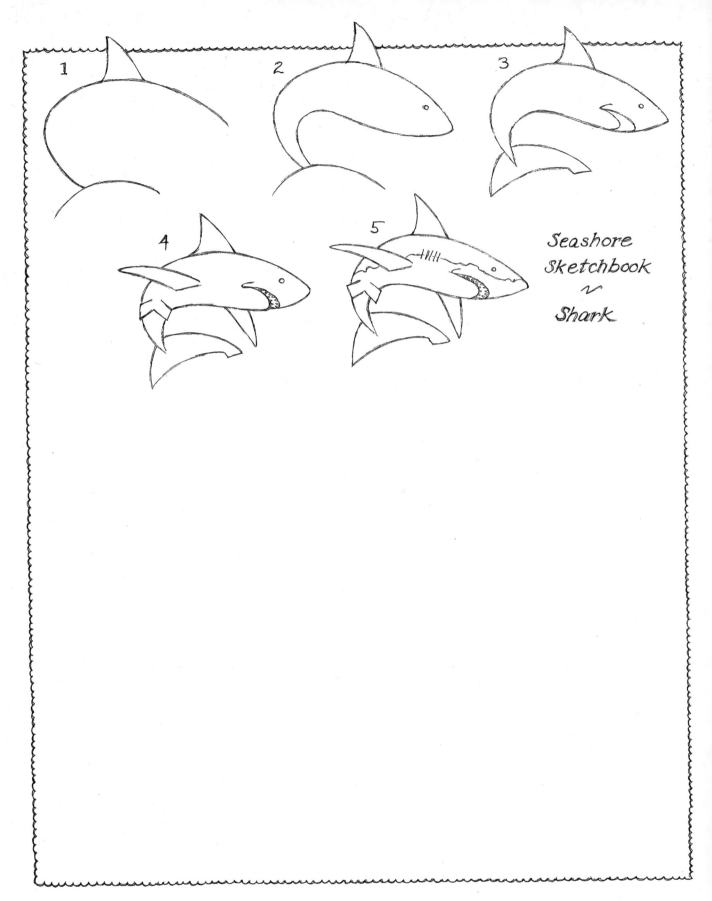

1

2

3

4

5

Seashore
Sketchbook
~
Shark

Great white sharks have rows of sharp teeth. When a tooth breaks, a new one grows in.
Draw your own great white shark. Color the shark gray and white.

 RI.1.1 Ask and answer questions about key details in a text. Also **RI.1.4, RI.1.6, RF.1.4, L.1.6; RI.2.1, RI.2.3, RI.2.4, RI.2.6, RF.2.4, L.2.6.**

Tide pools are miniature oceans. These pools have rockweed, snails, starfish, and urchins.
Circle eight things in the bottom pool that are different.

Starfish are always looking for food. They eat clams and scallops. Starfish come in different sizes. Can you spot the starfish on this page that is different?

 RI.1.2 Identify the main topic and retell key details of a text. Also **RI.1.1, RI.1.7, L.1.6; RI.2.1, RI.2.7, L.2.6.**

Sea horses like to be near seaweed. They also like clinging to rocks.
There are six sea horses hidden in the seaweed. Find and circle all six.

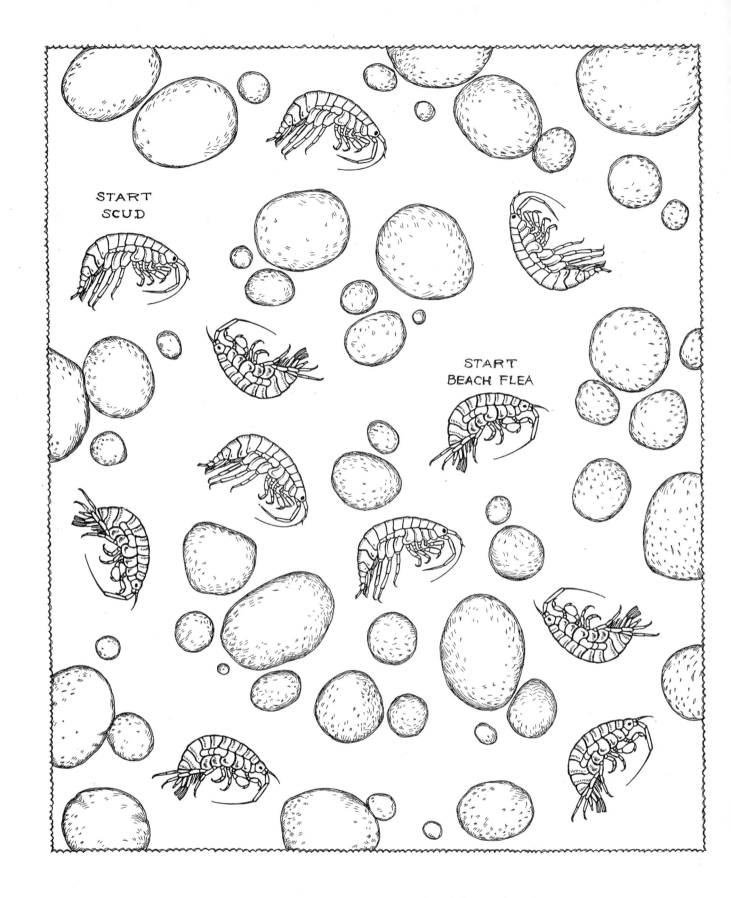

START
SCUD

START
BEACH FLEA

Look at the difference between the tiny beach fleas and scuds.
Connect all five scuds with a straight line. Then connect all six fleas. Avoid the pebbles as you draw.

 RI.1.1 Ask and answer questions about key details in a text. Also **RI.1.4, RI.1.5, RI.1.6; RI.2.1, RI.2.4, RI.2.5, RI.2.6.**

This is a giant kelp forest. It is home to many sea creatures.
Circle nine things different in the scene on the right.

RI.1.9 Identify basic similarities in and differences between two texts on the same topic.
Also **RI.1.4, RI.1.7, RF.1.4, SL.1.2; RI.2.4, RI.2.7, RI.2.9, RF.2.4, SL.2.2.**

The big channeled dogwinkle is looking to eat tiny periwinkle snails. Circle eight hiding periwinkles.

 RI.1.4 Ask and answer questions to help determine or clarify the meaning of words and phrases in a text. Also **RI.1.7, SL.1.2, L.1.4.c; RI.2.4, RI.2.7, SL.2.2.**

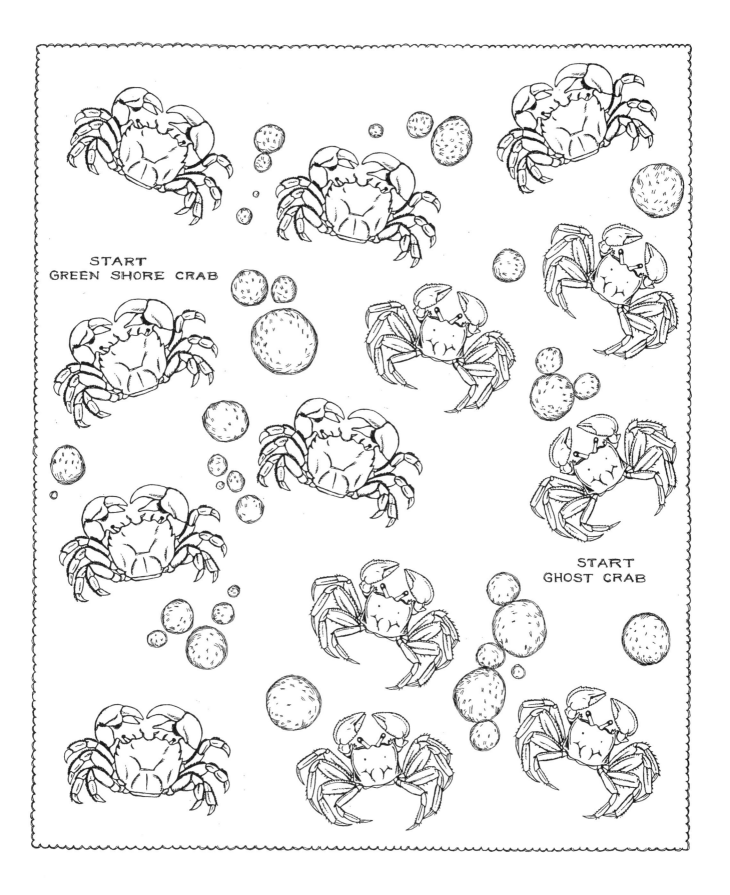

START
GREEN SHORE CRAB

START
GHOST CRAB

Crabs have ten legs and a hard shell. Using straight lines, connect seven green shore crabs.
Then connect six ghost crabs. Avoid the pebbles as you draw.

 RI.1.1 Ask and answer questions about key details in a text. Also **RI.1.5, RI.1.6, RF.1.4; RI.2.1, RI.2.5, RI.2.6, RF.2.4.**

PICTURE A

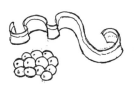
PICTURE B

PICTURE C

PICTURE D

PICTURE E

Every answer to the crossword puzzle is in this book—look carefully at the captions and the illustrations. Good luck!

ACROSS

1. The worm that shares its burrow is an _____.

2. A starfish hunts for _____ to eat.

3. There is always a lot of sand on the _____.

4. Answer this question. Is a sea horse really a horse?

5. The sea _____ isn't purple, like the fruit in its name.

6. This sea creature is a type of dollar, but it isn't money.

7. Picture B shows a group of _____ eggs.

8. Picture D shows a horned flat_____.

9. A mermaid's purse holds the egg of a _____.

10. The bone shown in Picture F is from a _____.

11. Picture G shows a _____.

12. The piping plover in this book has _____ eggs.

13. The seashore runs along the _____.

14. The whale shown in Picture H is a _____.

15. Picture I shows a harbor _____.

DOWN

A. A _____ worm grows to four feet long.

B. Sea otters can be found in _____ forests.

C. Some pelicans have _____ feathers.

D. The sea creature shown in Picture A is a _____.

E. The spike on a conch's foot is called an _____.

F. These creatures can be found in driftwood.

G. A conch has a foot, but it doesn't have a _____.

H. The flatworm in Picture C has a pair of _____ on its head.

I. This beetle has the same name as a big cat.

J. Picture E shows a sea _____.

K. A _____ cowrie is covered with spots.

L. A clam's siphon tubes pull water _____ and out of its shell.

M. You have drawn a picture of a Fighting _____ snail.

CCSS **RI.1.5** Know and use various text features to locate key facts or information in a text. Also **RI.1.1, RI.1.6, RF.1.4.a; RI.2.1, RI.2.5, RI.2.6, RF.2.4.a.**

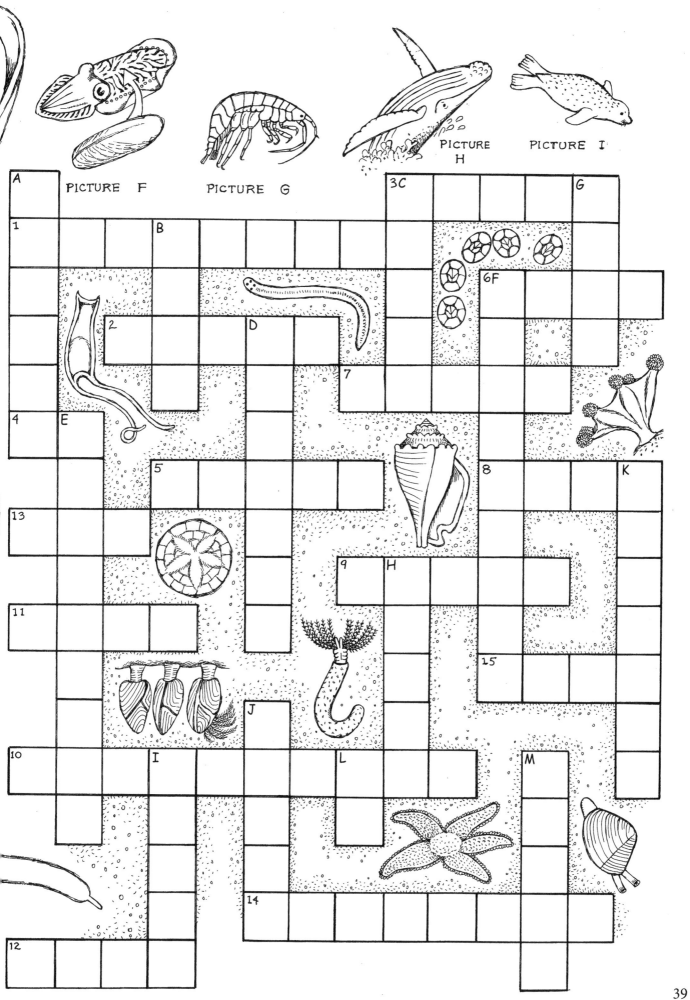

PICTURE F   PICTURE G   PICTURE H   PICTURE I

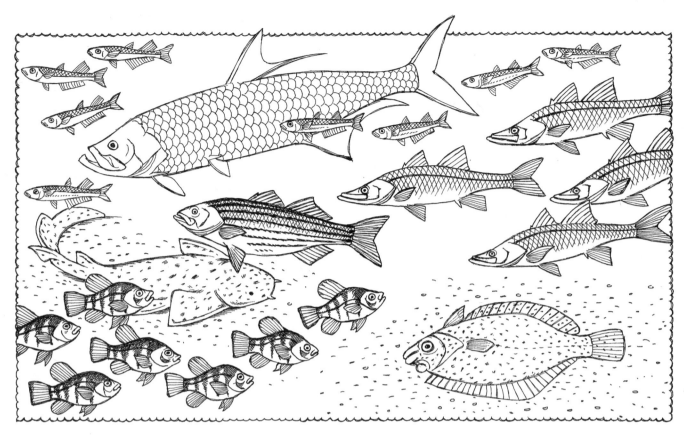

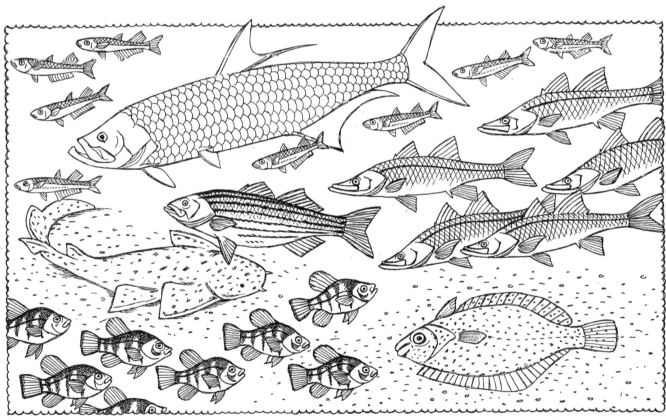

Fish swim in groups called "schools." The flounder and angel shark lie on the seafloor.
Circle eight things in the bottom scene that are different.

 RI.1.9 Identify basic similarities in and differences between two texts on the same topic.
Also **RI.1.1, RI.1.7, RI.1.10, L.1.6; RI.2.1, RI.2.7, RI.2.10, L.2.6.**

Solutions

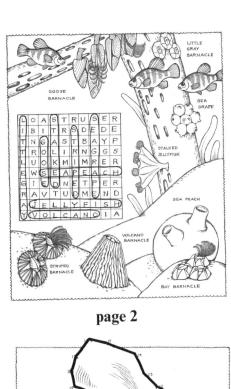

page 2

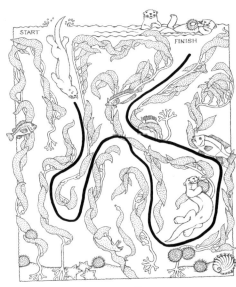

page 3

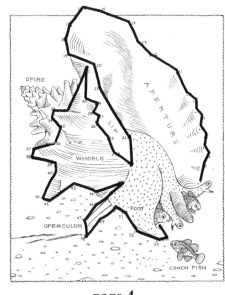

page 4

page 5

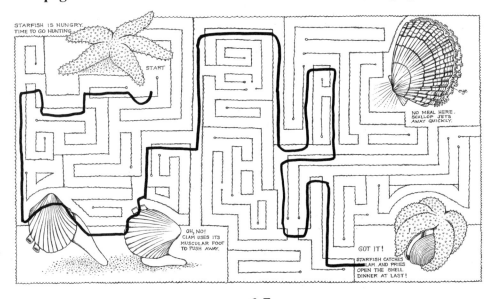

pages 6-7

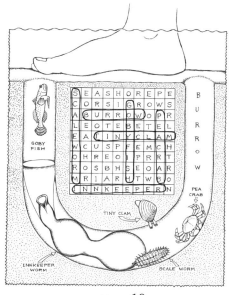

page 10

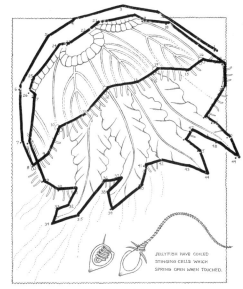

page 11

page 12-13

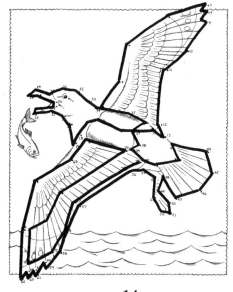

page 14

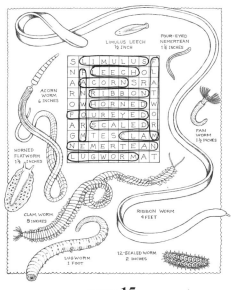

page 15

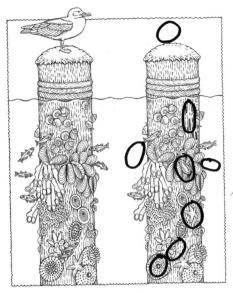

page 17

page 19

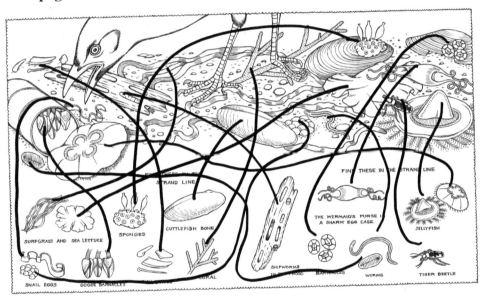

pages 20-21

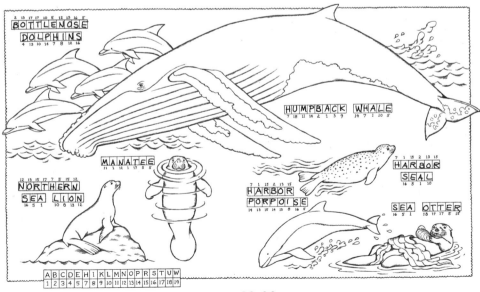

pages 22-23

page 24

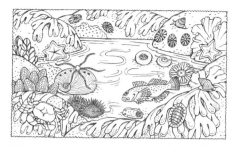

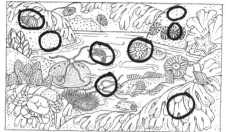

page 31

page 32

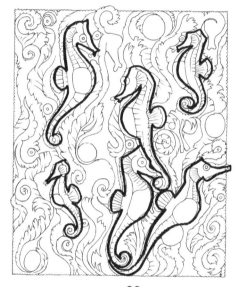

page 33

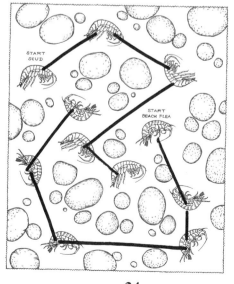

page 34

page 35

page 36

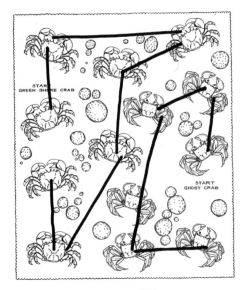

page 37

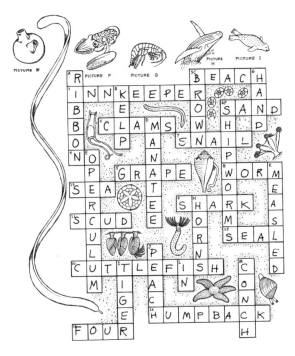

page 39

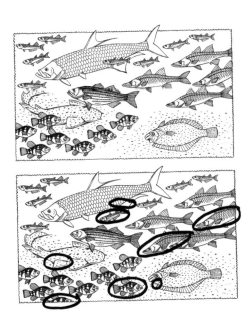

page 40